Hell and High Water

POEMS BY

WOLFGANG CARSTENS

Hell and High Water
Copyright 2017 © Wolfgang Carstens

Six Ft. Swells Press
www.AfterHoursPoetry.com
www.facebook.com/SixFtSwells

Editor: Todd Cirillo
Book & Cover Design: Julie Valin,
www.TheWordBoutique.net
Photograph on front cover: Matt Amott

Some of these poems have appeared in *Poems-For-All*.

All rights reserved.
Printed in the United States of America.
No part of this book may be reproduced in any manner without written permission except in the case of brief quotations included in critical essays, reviews and articles.

ISBN: 978-0-9853075-6-1

For Tracy Lee:

my alien princess,
my shining light,
my one true love.

you make me want to live

to the point of tears.

Contents

i wore.	11
it wasn't	12
Slave Lake, 2014	13
"i don't write love poems,"	14
instead of "Speed Bump,"	15
my wife	16
crooked quotes:	17
after drinking	18
the human animal	19
when	20
although	21
"you can't park there,"	22
jumping on the trampoline	23
the exterior	24
caught watching porn	25
i passed	26
it was.	28
Jerry	29
"Daddy,".	30
when Raven	31
Charles Bukowski	32
i bought myself	33
Tina Maria,	34
unable to build	36
Jeffery Dahmer	37
she's.	38
Len	39
"so,"	40
my wife	41
i brought my dog.	42
"look,".	43
contrary	44
Tracy Lee,	45

i was driving	46
"what does	47
i had a dream	48
my wife	49
i woke up	50
when Janey	52
the only things	53
about to leave	54
there's an old joke	55
in the doctor's office,	56
at the video arcade,	57
blank..	58
"if not a mess,"	59
she	60
strange	61

The Devil and The Deluge

Twenty-five years is a long time to stick with anything, let alone love. Yet, in *Hell and High Water* by Wolfgang Carstens, we are presented with a savage look into the essential life concepts of love, commitment, obligations, creativity, responsibilities, fatherhood, regret and the matrimonial benefits of good tequila. Carstens goes all in with these poems like a prize fighter in the final round of his career, showing the brutally beautiful and amusingly mundane of a champion poet surrounded by children, pets, current wife and exes, neighbors and bills.

Carstens masterly fulfills the responsibilities of a poet; to entertain, to present his version of truth and be not afraid. These poems betray signature moments when marriages are saved and moments when the question, "is it even worth saving?" must be asked. They offer a glimpse at intimate life with another person in terms of sex (or lack thereof), morning rituals, midnight worries and being so close together yet still feeling "a million miles away." Though humor runs throughout these poems, it is the tenderness and vulnerability that remain with the reader, whether this is by devil or design, *Hell and High Water* gives us panicked minutes of lost children, expensive trips to the vet with the dog, dishes to be cleaned, sparks that need a flame, and those neglected little moments that suddenly seem "worth dying for" when they disappear.

So, open a bottle of good tequila and take these poems to heart. There is a chance that Wolfgang Carstens may have just discovered some secrets to enduring love and creativity that he is generous enough, or drunk enough, to have put to paper as a twisted guide for the rest of us in maintaining the wildness among minivans, mortgages and matrimony for these next twenty-five years.

—Todd Cirillo, poet, editor
1:26am 9/30/17

i wore

a Trojan
"Fire and Ice"
condom.

it
was like
fucking
my prom date—

and
my wife

at
the same
time.

it wasn't

the wedding ring,
the crazy inlaws,
or not being able
to play poker
every Friday.

it wasn't even
having to drive
his daughters to ballet
three times a week.

it was
the
mini-van.

Slave Lake, 2014

we were on vacation.

my wife was mad at me.
she's always mad at me
about one thing or another.

we were at the beach.
she wanted to leave
and i wanted to fish.

she made her stand on the shore
with the kids and the dog.
i dragged my lawn chair
twenty feet in the water
and sat down.

come hell or high water,
i wasn't leaving.

i got both.

hell
and high water.

"i don't write love poems,"

i said,

"and i've never been
much of an Anglerfish."

"what does that even mean?"
my wife asked.

"well,"
i said,

"when Anglerfish mate,
they melt into each other.

the female absorbs her man,
until his eyes, mouth,
and fins disappear —

and they share
the same bloodstream."

"i like that,"
my wife says.

"well then,"
i say,

"come here Mama,

and let me
hold you

tighter."

instead of "Speed Bump,"

the sign read
"Speed Hump."

"look Honey,"
my wife said,
laughing.

"finally,

a sport
you
can win."

my wife

found
my cock ring

and made
a big deal
about it.

she
called me
shady,

pervert,

and
other names.

i honestly
don't think
she knows what
a cock ring
does

but still,
it could have
been worse—

she
could have found
the pump
that goes
with it.

crooked quotes:

"nasty,
brutish,
and short."

it took
me a minute
to realize
he'd said
"your life is"

and not
"your wife is."

after drinking

a bottle
of top shelf
Tequila,

my wife
started talking
about giving me
a blowjob.

it
got me thinking

we should really
drink Tequila

more often.

the human animal

possesses
an uncanny ability
to justify any action
after the fact:

if the devil
didn't make us do it,
we were drunk,
stoned
or temporarily
insane.

when all else fails,
we blame it
on love.

when

Karl's wife
passed away
unexpectedly

i
didn't know
whether
to send
my condolences,
my congratulations,

or
to ask
if he needed
help

with
an alibi.

although

it was
minus forty,

he
was outside
smoking.

he
had been
married
so long

the cold
no longer
bothered
him.

"you can't park there,"

Lexi said,

"the sign says
this spot is reserved
for pregnant
or expecting mothers."

"don't
worry about it,"

my wife hissed,

"i may not be
pregnant,

but

i am fully
expecting
all of you

to behave
like jackasses

once we get
inside."

jumping on the trampoline

with my seventeen year-old daughter
and her boyfriend Matt,
playing "crack the egg"
with our younger children,

my wife
jumped so hard
her pants came down
and her fat ass
went into Matt's face.

"take a good look
at your future,"
she joked.

the next day
Krissy and Matt broke up.

i wonder
what happened.

the exterior

of the *Svensk Apache*
translation
of my poetry
reminds me
of a Frank Miller
nightmare.

Janne Karlsson
has captured
the inner landscape
of my mind
perfectly.

now,
when my wife
sarcastically remarks
"i want to vacation
in Wolfgang Land,"
at least she'll know
exactly
where she's going.

"it's dark,
oppressive,
gloomy,

and baby,

you'll fit
right in
with the
locals."

caught watching porn

"well,

i guess you'll
have to use
your imagination
now,"

she hissed,

opening the lid
and dropping
my laptop
into
the toilet.

i passed

my wife
in the kitchen
this morning
as i usually do,

without touching.

i made myself a coffee,
then put my arms around her
and gave her the biggest hug.

i kissed her neck,
her cheek,
ears,
lips,

and whispered
"i love you Mama."

it was so simple,
this small act of kindness
and it changed her day
and mine.

later, she texted me
"that was a great hug Baby.
thank you."

as i think about it,
if we are lucky enough
to have another 25 years
together,

i will remember this hug

and say
it was the moment
that saved

our marriage.

it was

a nice gesture,
of course,

getting
the heart tattoo

with his name
inked across it,

but,
in his heart
of hearts,

he knew
she had it
backwards.

it was he
that would always
belong

to
her.

Jerry

wasn't sure
if it had been
a Freudian slip

or not.

all
he knew
was
it had
a nice ring
to it:

killdren.

"Daddy,"

Raven says,

"why
do you sit

fishing
for hours,

not catching
anything?"

"Honey,"

i say,

"do you
see

your mother
here?"

"no,"
she says.

"exactly,"

i say.

when Raven

was lost in the woods
and nobody could find her,
i came very close
to praying
to an imaginary god
for help.

that

is what
hurts me
the
most.

Charles Bukowski

instructed us
to find
what we love

and
let it
kill us.

i have been
happily married
twenty-five years

to
an apex
predator —

and
every day
with her

is
a good
day

to die.

i bought myself

a year's subscription
of adult toys.

every month
they send me
something new.

the last four
have been
dildos.

it's only May

and
frankly,

i don't know
how much more

my ass

can
take.

Tina Maria,

my first wife,
always
needed to be
the center
of attention.

i ran into her
a few years ago.

she mentioned
that she had been
following my career.

"i've read
your poems
about Alice,
Sandra Dawn,
and Tracy Lee,"
she said.

"have you
written any poems
about me,"
she asked.

"no,"
i said.

the look
on her face
was priceless.

i guess it's true.

revenge
really is a dish
best served
cold.

unable to build

a fire
with flint and steel,

he turned to me
and said,

"if

i wanted
to spend the night
shivering,

i would have
stayed home
with
my wife."

Jeffery Dahmer

was right.

the
best way
to a man's
heart

is

through his
stomach.

she's

in
the other room

but
it feels

a
million miles
away.

Len

always thought
the *iwantmycarpetcleaned.com* van
that he'd seen
driving around town
was fucking hilarious.

that is,
until the day
he came home
early from work
and found it
parked
in his driveway.

"so,"

my wife asked,

"what
would you
like
for dessert?"

i
pushed
the half-eaten
pork chop
around
my plate,

laughed,

then said,

"the
antidote."

my wife

asked
for some dirty
pictures

so

i texted her
photos
of the
kitchen.

i brought my dog

to the vet yesterday
for a check-up.

when he jammed
the thermometer
up her ass,

she started
getting antsy.

"relax,"
i told her.

"this
is costing $117.

at least
try
to enjoy it."

"look,"

i said,
with fifteen
coffee cups
dangling from my fingers,

"some dumb bastard
put all our dishes
in the van."

"yeah,"
my wife quipped,

"and now
some stupid bitch
has to wash them."

contrary

to popular music,

it's never
better to burn out
than to fade away,

love
isn't all you
need,

and

time
is never
on our side.

Tracy Lee,

i know

your hands
and feet
are sore.

i know
you have
trouble
breathing.

i know
life
is tough
for you.

but baby
we belong together

and

i mean
no disrespect
when i say

all i want
is you
naked

on your hands
and knees

with my hands
around your hips

pulling you

into
me.

i was driving

with a cigarette in one hand,
a cup of coffee in the other,

steering with two fingers,

all the while
eating sunflower seeds.

"wow Honey,"
i said,

"i should get
some kind of award
for driving like this."

"yeah,"
my wife agreed,

"it's called
a ticket."

"what does

Reposada mean,"

my wife asked.

"i don't know
for sure,"

i said,

"but
i think it means

blowjob."

i had a dream

that my wife
woke me
saying "let's fuck."

i opened my eyes,
rolled over
and found her
fast asleep.

so
i clicked on the TV,
lit a cigarette
and watched a re-run
of Married With Children.

as she lay there,
snoring like a bloody lumberjack,
i muttered
"fuck you Peg."

my wife

wakes me
early

to drive her
to work.

"i was
in the middle
of a gorgeous
dream,"

i complain.

"what's more important,"
she asks,

"your dreams
or driving me
to work?"

i haven't
the heart
to tell her

that after
twenty-five years
of marriage

all
i have left
are my

dreams.

i woke up

in the middle
of the night.

i
couldn't breathe,

my heart
was beating out
of my chest,

and our bed
was a teacup ride
at the carnival.

the room
smelled of
Death.

i put
my head
in your lap

and
it calmed me.

i fell asleep
and woke
with this poem.

and
i wanted you
to know

you saved me
last night,

my love.

you saved me.

when Janey

up
and left
John's sorry ass,

all those
piddly-shit
errands
she
was always
making him
run
for her

suddenly

seemed
worth
dying
for.

the only things

biting
at the Cline
River

~~were~~

the mosquitoes,
the horseflies,

and

my
wife's
sarcasm.

about to leave

she turned

and said,
"this
is what love
looks like."

for once

i
couldn't
argue.

there's an old joke

that goes

when
Ronnie James Dio
arrived at the mouth
of Hell,

he looked at Satan,
grinned,
then said,
"you're in my seat."

now,
this well may be true,

but Dio,
mark my words,

enjoy it
while you can

because soon enough,

my wife
will arrive
at your doorstep

to kick you

out.

in the doctor's office,

my wife
kept talking nonsense,
interrupting,
and making a nuisance
of herself.

"unfortunately,
without understanding
the root cause,
there's nothing
that can be done
about your migraines,"
the doctor said.

he wrote me a prescription
for painkillers

then,
as we were leaving
and my wife
was well out of earshot,
he added,

"between you,
me, and the wall
i have a pretty good idea
what's causing your headaches,

and
the only prescription
is a good
lawyer."

at the video arcade,

instead of a game token,
the change machine
spit out
a peepshow coin
with the letters
S-E-X
engraved on it.

"maybe tonight
is my lucky night,"
i said,
showing the coin
to my wife.

boy,
was i

wrong.

blank.

blank. blank.
blank. blank. blank.
blank.

you.

blank. blank.
blank. blank. blank.
blank.

it's always
you.

"if not a mess,"

my wife groaned,

as she picked up
the empty Tequila bottles
the empty beer cans
and
the half-smoked joint,

"then
what do you call it?"

"we
have been married
twenty-five years,"

i said,
lighting the joint,

"and that,
my Dear,

is what
i call

a survival
kit."

she

calls me
"Mr. Right."

i
call her
"Mrs. Always
Right."

it's not
a perfect
relationship

but

it's
close.

strange.

it's not
the big moments
in life
that terrify us,

but rather,
the small,
ordinary ones.

i can stand
in front of 300 people
and read poetry,

yet,
my knees shake

when
i lean in close

and
kiss you

goodnight.

About the Author

Wolfgang Carstens lives in Canada with his wife, five kids, grandson, dog, mortgage and death. His poetry is printed on the backs of unpaid bills. More information at *www.wolfgangcarstens.com*.

Support the independent press
and After-Hours poetry!

visit Six Ft. Swells at
www.AfterHoursPoetry.com

and

Epic Rites Press
http://www.epicrites.org/

www.ingramcontent.com/pod-product-compliance
Lightning Source LLC
Chambersburg PA
CBHW051716040426
42446CB00008B/913